83-0608

PETROLEUM PRICE REGULATION

83-0608

HD 9565.6 .A77	Arrow, Kenneth Joseph, 1921- Petroleum price regulation

D1572417

SHAMBAUGH LIBRARY

GEORGE FOX COLLEGE

NEWBERG, OREGON 97132

PETROLEUM PRICE REGULATION

SHOULD WE DECONTROL?

**Kenneth J. Arrow and
Joseph P. Kalt**

Shambaugh Library

American Enterprise Institute for Public Policy Research
Washington, D.C.

HD
9565.6
.A77
X

Kenneth J. Arrow is Joan Kenney Professor of Economics at Stanford University. Joseph P. Kalt is an instructor of economics at Harvard University.

ISBN 0-8447-3359-8

Library of Congress Catalog Card No. 79-8830

AEI Studies 256

© 1979 by American Enterprise Institute for Public Policy Research, Washington, D.C. All rights reserved. No part of this publication may be used or reproduced in any manner whatsoever without permission in writing from the American Enterprise Institute except in the case of brief quotations embodied in news articles, critical articles, or reviews.

The views expressed in the publications of the American Enterprise Institute are those of the authors and do not necessarily reflect the views of the staff, advisory panels, officers, or trustees of AEI.

"American Enterprise Institute" is the registered service mark of the American Enterprise Institute for Public Policy Research.

Printed in the United States of America

CONTENTS

1

Introduction

The consequences of any change in a regulatory policy can be classi-
fied into two general categories according to the questions such
consequences pose for policy makers.

- First, any change in the regulatory environment of the economy
typically changes the constraints and opportunities faced both by
consumers and by producers. The results are alterations in behavior
that ultimately affect production costs, market prices, and the allocation of resources among their many alternative uses. These allocative
effects of regulation raise important questions of *efficiency*. That is,
the well-meaning policy maker must consider whether the benefits of
any proposed change in regulatory policy and reallocation of resources
exceed or fall short of the costs.
- Second, any allocative impacts of changes in regulation are
typically accompanied by changes in the distributions of income and
rights to action in the economy. These distributional effects of regulation raise important questions of *equity*. That is, the well-meaning
policy maker must consider whether any proposed change in regulatory policy is just and proper.

These two types of questions are as pertinent to energy policy
decisions as they are to any other issue of public policy.

Consider, for example, a policy proposing to mandate that all
homeowners who burn home heating oil keep their thermostat set-
tings below, say, 60°F. Such a requirement would have subtle, yet
certain, allocative effects. The demand for home heating oil would
decline, and petroleum freed from use as home heating oil could be
turned into other forms of fuel and applied to activities other than
keeping people warm. At the same time, the demand and, hence,

1

the price paid for houses in warm climates, solar-heating equipment, and even sweaters and blankets would increase. These changes would immediately raise issues of efficiency: Is the value of the saving of home heating oil greater than the value of the resources used up in finding alternative methods of providing society with warmth? Moreover, these induced changes in the public's behavior would have distributional consequences—although these effects might be even more subtle than the allocative consequences. The proposed policy would be a boon, for example, to the sellers of sun-belt homes, solar equipment, sweaters, and blankets. But the proposed policy would adversely affect the well-being of the sellers of home heating oil, as well as the families forced to turn down their thermostats and to find other means of satisfying their wants. Are those who would benefit from the proposed policy more deserving than those who would be harmed? Is it proper to restrict the rights of homeowners to allocate their incomes as they see fit? Although equity questions of these types may be explicitly addressed and resolved only rarely in policy debates, answers to them are implicit in every regulatory decision.

Of course, public policy changes are not the only source of economic shocks that have allocative and distributional effects. Some shocks may originate from sources beyond the control of policy makers and may induce calls for a regulatory response. Perhaps the most notable recent instance of such a shock from outside sources was the quadrupling of world oil prices through the actions of the Organization of Petroleum Exporting Countries (OPEC) in the first half of the 1970s. This event signaled major changes in domestic energy markets. The dramatic rise in petroleum prices and the prices of energy forms that are substitutes for petroleum has portended major changes in consumption and production patterns—toward a more conservative use of energy in general and an expansion of the output of energy forms that are alternatives to OPEC oil. At the same time, the energy price increases of this decade have portended a substantial redistribution of income from the intermediate and final users of primary energy to the producers of primary energy.

In response to the energy developments of the 1970s, policy makers have undertaken a major expansion of the role of governmental regulation in the energy sector. This regulation has included the introduction of measures such as the subsidization of less energy-intensive consumption patterns, voluntary and mandatory standards for energy conservation, and public support of research and development in alternative supply technologies. In terms of the magnitude

2

of both allocative and distributional effects, however, the most important component of energy policy in this era of rising world energy prices has been the attempt to constrain domestic price increases with elaborate systems of price controls on natural gas and petroleum.

Both natural-gas and petroleum price controls are appropriate subjects for in-depth analyses. In the case of natural gas, domestic production has been subject to some form of price regulation since 1954. The consequences of this regulation, however, did not attract widespread attention for many years. Then, with rising world energy prices and rapid inflation in the early and mid-1970s, fixed price ceilings on natural gas sold in interstate commerce caused dramatic and disruptive shortages in net consuming states. Under the pressure of these severe allocative distortions and competing distributional interests, the Natural Gas Policy Act of 1978 was eventually hammered out. This act *extended* federal price ceilings to previously uncontrolled intrastate markets and created an extremely complicated set of new regulations with more than twenty categories of controlled gas.

Despite the questionable value of current natural-gas policy, this morass of regulation is not the most pressing immediate concern of policy makers. It is not likely that our political institutions are prepared to take up the issue of natural-gas pricing so soon after the recent rounds of heated debate. This is not the situation, however, with petroleum price controls. Current legislation mandates that a series of important policy decisions be made over the next several years. This creates the opportunity for a fundamental rethinking of U.S. energy policy.

This study examines the allocative and distributional effects of energy price regulation and addresses the issues of both efficiency and equity in the domestic pricing of energy. The primary focus here is the regulation of petroleum prices—although the general character of the analysis is applicable to natural-gas price controls as well. Issues of equity arise in the policy debate over the regulation of petroleum prices because current regulations have forbidden the producers of crude oil from selling their output at market prices; and because current regulations have forestalled much of the prospective transfer of wealth from domestic energy users to domestic energy producers, which would otherwise accompany rising world prices for energy. Issues of efficiency arise because constraining this transfer via the economy's pricing mechanisms distorts energy use and production decisions.

This study finds that current regulation of the petroleum industry causes significant inefficiency in our use of resources. This inefficiency is a real cost for the economy and is not offset by real economic benefits. A significant portion of the costs of current price controls arises from the underproduction of domestic petroleum and over-consumption of imported petroleum induced by artificially low prices. Substantial costs are also associated with impairments to the economy's ability to adjust to sharp increases in world energy prices, the implicit regulatory support for the OPEC cartel and its pricing objectives, and the administration and enforcement of present policies. The avoidance of all of these costs by moving to an uncontrolled market would represent a major source of gain to the nation. Of course, such a policy change would have distributional consequences that might be regarded as inequitable. Even with assumptions that are generous to such a judgment, however, the case is strong that decontrol of petroleum prices would be preferable to the current policy. This conclusion emerges because the regressiveness and magnitude of the net redistributions of income that would occur under decontrol would be mollified by certain attributes of current regulation and tax policy. Still, those who object to these prospective redistributions would want to accompany decontrol with a windfall-profits tax, the proceeds of which accrue to the Treasury's general revenues.

2

The Petroleum Price Regulations

The oil embargo of 1973 prompted the passage of the comprehensive Emergency Petroleum Allocation Act (EPAA). A major provision of EPAA was the extension of the two-tier pricing system for domestically marketed crude oil, which had originally been implemented by the Cost of Living Council in August 1973. The crude-oil pricing regulations of EPAA were superseded in February 1976 by the provisions of the Energy Policy and Conservation Act of 1975 (EPCA). EPCA established a three-tier pricing program for domestically marketed crude oil and is scheduled to remain in effect through September 1981. In accord with EPCA regulations, the President has recently exercised his power to begin the decontrol of crude-oil prices in June 1979. The President's plan calls for a gradual lifting of price ceilings until decontrol is reached on October 1, 1981, but this plan has been challenged and apparently will continue to be challenged in Congress. It remains to be seen whether gradual decontrol will be blocked and whether EPCA will be followed by new control legislation in 1981. For the purposes of comparing controlled and uncontrolled regimes in this study, we primarily concern ourselves with the pricing regulations as they would exist if the decontrol begun in June 1979 were blocked (or had not begun) and the alternative of complete decontrol.

Tables 1 and 2 summarize EPCA pricing. There are three price tiers under EPCA: lower, upper, and uncontrolled. Under EPCA regulations, each oil field that began production by 1975 is given a base level of output determined in a complicated way by production levels prior to 1976. All production up to this base level is defined as "lower-tier" crude oil. Output in excess of the lower-tier base level and from fields not producing prior to 1976 is defined as

TABLE 1

DOMESTIC CRUDE-OIL PRICES, 1976–1979

(dollars per barrel at the wellhead)

	Lower Tier	Upper Tier	Stripper[b]	Alaskan North Slope[c]	Naval Petroleum Reserve[d]
1976 average[a]	5.14	11.59	12.08	–	–
1977 average	5.19	11.22	13.59	6.35	12.34
1978 average	5.46	12.15	13.95	5.22	12.85
1979 January	5.75	12.66	14.55	5.79	13.08
February	5.76	12.78	14.88	5.87	13.94
March	5.82	12.84	14.88	6.66	13.47
April	5.85	12.94	16.71	7.45	14.56
May	5.91	13.01	17.54	8.51	15.56

[a] Average for February 1976 (when the Energy Policy and Conservation Act of 1975 went into effect) through December 1976.

[b] From February 1976 through August 1976, stripper oil was subject to upper-tier price ceilings. Since September 1976, stripper oil has been exempt from price controls.

[c] Alaskan North Slope crude-oil prices were reported as Upper Tier prior to July 1977.

[d] The federally owned Naval Petroleum Reserves are exempt from price controls, but were reported as Upper Tier prior to July 1977.

SOURCE: Calculated from U.S. Department of Energy, *Monthly Energy Review*.

"upper-tier" crude oil. Oil fields that produce an average of less than ten barrels per well per day are said to produce "stripper" oil. Lower-tier oil is subject to a federal price ceiling of $5.03 per barrel plus small monthly incentive and inflation adjustment factors determined by the Department of Energy. Upper-tier oil is subject to a ceiling of $11.28 plus monthly adjustment factors. Alaskan North Slope crude oil is also subject to an upper-tier ceiling, but large transportation costs keep its wellhead price below this level. Stripper oil, federally owned oil, and imported oil are free from price controls and sell at market-determined prices. Suppliers of price-controlled domestic crude oil are required to continue to sell oil to customers who bought it before controls were in effect.

Under both EPAA and EPCA, the prices of refined petroleum products have been subject to controls that limit prices in any month to 1973 base levels plus dollar-for-dollar adjustments to allow for changes in average production costs. During 1976, however, all

TABLE 2
DOMESTIC PRODUCTION BY CONTROL CATEGORY
(percent)

	Lower Tier	Upper Tier	Stripper	Alaskan North Slope	Naval Petroleum Reserve
1976 average	54.4	31.6	14.0	–	–
1977 average	45.9	36.1	13.3	4.1	0.5
1978 average	37.5	34.4	14.0	13.0	1.1
1979 January	35.5	34.3	14.1	14.9	1.1
February	35.2	35.0	15.1	13.7	1.0
March	34.6	34.6	15.0	14.6	1.3
April	34.0	34.9	15.3	14.5	1.3
May	33.5	34.7	15.6	14.8	1.3

NOTE: See notes to Table 1. Percentages may not add to 100 because of rounding.
SOURCE: Calculated from U.S. Department of Energy, *Monthly Energy Review*.

major refined products except gasoline and jet fuel became exempt from price controls. Jet fuel became exempt in early 1979.

In the absence of some program that equalizes refiners' costs, a multitier pricing system for crude oil would result in differences in the average per barrel cost of crude oil to refiners. Thus, a refiner granted access (through the regulatory freezing of buyer–supplier relationships) to relatively large amounts of crude oil that is subject to price controls would have lower average costs of production than a refiner whose only source of supply is the uncontrolled market for imported and stripper crude oil. As a result, crude-oil price regulation, coupled with a freezing of buyer–supplier relationships, would tend to cause disparities in the profits of refiners.

The entitlements program adopted by the Federal Energy Administration in November 1974 has the effect of making the average cost of crude oil more nearly equal for all refiners. Under this program, the Department of Energy makes monthly issues of "entitlements" to controlled crude oil to each refiner. The number of entitlements granted to any given refiner is equal to the number of barrels of controlled crude oil that the refiner would have used had it operated using the national average proportions of controlled and uncontrolled crude oil. If a refiner has used more controlled crude oil than the number of entitlements issued to it—that is, if it has used a higher proportion of controlled crude oil than the national average—that refiner's average crude-oil costs are lower than the national average of all refiners. Such a refiner must purchase entitlements from entitlements-selling refiners. If a refiner has processed fewer barrels of controlled crude oil than the number of entitlements it is issued, that refiner's average crude-oil costs are greater than the national average, and it is permitted to sell entitlements to entitlements-purchasing refiners. The purchase price of an entitlement is set at approximately the difference (less 21 cents) between the price of uncontrolled imported crude oil and the price of lower-tier crude oil.[1]

Requirements to buy entitlements increase the average production costs of refiners using relatively large amounts of lower priced, controlled crude oil. Requirements to sell entitlements, on the other hand, decrease the costs of refiners using relatively large amounts of higher priced, uncontrolled crude oil. By setting the number of entitlements appropriately, the Department of Energy can equalize the average crude-oil costs of all refiners. It is as if ownership of controlled crude oil were allocated proportionally among all refiners, because being granted an entitlement is tantamount to owning a barrel of controlled crude—although physical possession may never occur.

In fact, however, entitlements to controlled oil are not granted so as to equalize exactly refiners' average crude-oil costs. Many special programs are now built into the entitlements regulations. Smaller refiners (with capacity of less than 175,000 barrels per day), for example, are given a special subsidy in the form of extra allocations of salable entitlements. Importers of heavy industrial fuel oil also receive special allocations of salable entitlements, while numerous "exceptions and appeals" to entitlements obligations are granted to fortunate refiners. Finally, the federal government allocates itself salable entitlements in order to lower the average cost of its Strategic Petroleum Reserve Plan, under which crude oil is stored as insurance against supply disruptions.

---

[1] The 21 cent allowance derives from a 21 cent preference for domestic oil embodied in the U.S. import fee program. The 21 cent import fee, in the absence of domestic price controls, would accrue to domestic crude-oil producers in the form of higher wellhead prices. The 21 cent adjustment in the entitlements obligation was justified on the grounds that it maintains incentives for refining domestic crude oil. See James C. Cox and Arthur W. Wright, "The Effects of Crude Oil Price Controls, Entitlements and Taxes on Refined Product Prices and Energy Independence," *Land Economics*, February 1978, p. 6.

3

Regulation and Efficiency

The Costs of Controls and Entitlements:
Inefficiency on the Demand Side

Domestic crude-oil price controls prevent much of the increase in the wealth of crude-oil producers which would otherwise result from a raising of domestic prices to world levels. An estimate of this potential increase in wealth can be made by calculating the difference between the revenues that would be generated at observed production levels in the absence of controls and the actual revenues from the sale of controlled crude oil. Assuming that EPAA/EPCA legislation has no impact on the world price of crude oil, these potential transfers have averaged approximately $13–14 billion per year over the last several years. With the decline of domestic production and a narrowing of the gap between world and domestic prices, these potential transfers fell to approximately $11 billion in 1978. In 1979, however, sharp increases in world oil prices have raised this figure substantially. Based on data for May 1979 (the month before the President began gradual decontrol) which reflect a large part of this year's rise in world prices, EPCA controls would currently be restraining the revenues of crude-oil producers on actual output at an annual rate (if decontrol were blocked) of approximately $17 billion.[1]

---

[1] Data are from the U.S. Department of Energy, *Monthly Energy Review.* Throughout this study, the current effects of controls are expressed as annual rates estimated on the basis of May 1979 data. Several considerations have dictated this approach. First, because our object is to compare the results that would obtain in an uncontrolled setting with those that would obtain if decontrol is blocked and EPCA regulations are retained in their pre-June 1979 status, May 1979 data provide the most up-to-date picture of the latter set of circumstances. Second, May 1979 data reflect the bulk of the rise in world oil prices in early 1979. Third, complete data from official sources are not yet available for months after May 1979.

These sums represent a boon to users of crude oil. Division of this windfall among these users (including large refiners, small refiners, and ultimate consumers such as businesses, utilities, and individuals) depends on the impact of the entitlements program. In the absence of an entitlements program, for example, refiners granted access to price-controlled domestic crude oil through the freezing of buyer–supplier relationships would capture the entire $17 billion annual transfer being generated in 1979—without having to pass any of their lower crude-oil costs through to final consumers. This conclusion may seem surprising. It might appear that, without the entitlements program, some refiners would operate with lower average production costs and, consequently, would be able to undersell their competitors—to the benefit of consumers. The pricing and supply decisions of any profit-seeking enterprise, however, are based upon the *incremental* cost of additional output rather than the average costs of particular output levels. The relevant question faced by any business firm is: Does the sale of one more unit of output give additional (incremental) revenue which exceeds the additional (incremental) cost of producing one more unit? If incremental revenue exceeds incremental cost, then an additional sale adds something to profits. If incremental revenue is less than incremental cost, profits are obviously reduced by an additional sale.

Even though average crude-oil costs would differ from one refiner to another in the absence of an entitlements program, the crude-oil cost that would be relevant for all refiners to the calculation of the incremental cost of refined-product output is the price of uncontrolled (primarily imported) crude oil—just as it would be in the absence of any federal regulation of the crude-oil market. This world-determined price is the relevant cost to refiners because domestic output of crude oil is insufficient to satisfy demand at controlled prices. Incremental units of refined-product output by any refiner require the use of uncontrolled crude oil. Thus, in the absence of an entitlements program, all refiners face essentially equal incremental costs even though their average crude oil costs are unequal.

The incremental revenue that is relevant to the decision to refine an additional barrel of crude oil is the sum of the prices actually received in the marketplace for those refined products that result from the additional crude oil. Apparently since early 1974 and the end of the long lines of customers in the refined-product markets, and certainly since 1976 and the removal of most product price controls, these refined-product prices have been set predominantly by the marketplace rather than by regulation. An exception to this conclusion developed in gasoline markets in the spring and summer of 1979, when ceiling prices again constrained market prices and created shortages reminiscent of the shortages created by controls in early 1974. In an uncontrolled market for refined products, the rivalry among refiners and the shrewdness of customers in seeking the best available prices result in approximately uniform prices for refined products. These prices, moreover, tend to be just sufficient to cover the cost of incremental output. No refiner could profit by attempting to increase sales through price reductions below this level because to do so would yield incremental revenues less than incremental costs.

In short, the incremental cost of crude oil for *all* refiners under a system of crude-oil price controls without entitlements would be the price of uncontrolled crude oil. Similarly, incremental revenues would be equal for *all* refiners and sufficient to cover incremental costs. Fortunate refiners with access to controlled crude oil would be able to refine barrels of such oil and sell the resulting output at prices high enough to cover the cost of their incremental products produced from uncontrolled crude oil. That is, refiners with access to controlled crude oil would be able to sell that crude oil, after transforming it into refined petroleum, on an equal basis with uncontrolled oil. Thus, refiners with access to controlled crude oil would receive windfall gains by buying crude oil at controlled prices. The windfall gain on each barrel of this "pre-incremental" crude oil would be equal to the difference between the price of uncontrolled crude oil and the price of controlled crude oil. The sum of these differences has been accumulating at an annual rate of approximately $17 billion in mid-1979.

The prospect of a transfer of $17 billion per year induces political competition for its acquisition among producers, refiners, and consumers. The entitlements program is an outcome of this process of competition and is the mechanism by which eventual ownership of the windfall gains that arise under crude-oil price controls is resolved. Under the entitlements program, the primary method by which a refiner tries to capture these gains is through the use of greater than normal amounts of uncontrolled crude oil.[2] If it is currently producing with a greater proportion of uncontrolled crude oil than the national average, a refiner can attempt to capture the windfall gains of other refiners by expanding its use of uncontrolled

[2] Controlled crude-oil output is insufficient to satisfy refiner demand at controlled prices. Hence, incremental supplies must be purchased in the uncontrolled market.

crude oil. Such a refiner thereby becomes eligible for a greater number of entitlements and greater payments for those entitlements from entitlements-purchasing refiners. Consequently, the effective cost of incremental crude oil to such a refiner is the uncontrolled price *minus* the increase in receipts from the sale of entitlements. On the other hand, if it is currently producing with a smaller proportion of uncontrolled crude oil than the average refiner, a refiner can attempt to retain its own windfall gains by expanding its use of uncontrolled crude oil, moving its proportions of controlled and uncontrolled crude oil closer to the national averages, and thereby reducing the burden of required entitlements purchases. Thus, the effective cost of the incremental barrel of crude oil to such a refiner is the uncontrolled price *minus* the incremental reduction in the burden of required entitlements purchases.

Under the entitlements program, then, *all* refiners perceive the cost of using one more barrel of crude oil as being less than the market price of the incremental barrel. This decline in incremental crude-oil costs caused by the entitlements program makes expanded production more profitable. Thus, refiners expand their use of crude oil and their output of refined petroleum products so long as their perceived incremental costs do not exceed the sum of the prices received for the incremental products in the market for refined petroleum products. In other words, the entitlements program, coupled with crude-oil price controls, has the same impact as a program of direct subsidies to refining. In fact, it is as if the Department of Energy taxes the windfall gains created by controls away from refiners and redistributes them as subsidies for the expansion of refinery output through the use of uncontrolled crude oil. Furthermore, because incremental supplies of uncontrolled crude oil primarily consist of imported oil, the entitlements program acts as a subsidy for the use of foreign oil.

The magnitude of the entitlements subsidy varies with the gap between the world price of oil and the national weighted-average price. An approximation of the magnitude of the subsidy can be made by considering that the entitlements program assures each refiner that the purchase of an incremental barrel of uncontrolled crude oil will be accompanied by either a reduction in its obligation to purchase or an increase in its opportunity to sell entitlements that is just large enough to reduce the cost of the incremental crude oil to the national weighted average. The difference in the refiner's acquisition cost of imported oil and the average cost of all domestically refined oil—a measure of the maximum possible entitlements subsidy—was $3.55 in

1975, $2.59 in 1976, $2.57 in 1977, and $2.11 in 1978, and it reached $3.56 in May 1979. Actual subsidies, however, were $2.84 in 1975, $2.51 in 1976, $2.27 in 1977, $1.60 in 1978, and $2.44 in May 1979.[3]

The differences between the maximum subsidies and the actual subsidies have been distributed through the program's bias toward small refiners, the special subsidy to industrial fuel importers, the "exceptions and appeals" process, the subsidy to the Strategic Petroleum Reserve, and an exemption from the entitlements program of a portion (21 cents per barrel) of the windfall gain associated with a refiner's access to controlled crude oil. Even with these special modifications of the entitlements program, actual subsidies have typically been paying for approximately one-tenth to one-fifth of each barrel of imported crude oil.

The effects of the entitlements subsidy on the refining industry are shown in Figure 1. The demand, D, of domestic refiners for crude oil is derived from the consumer demand for petroleum products. The price a refiner is willing to pay for crude oil (as shown by the height of D) is a measure of the amount consumers are willing to pay for the contribution that additional crude oil makes to the value of additional refined-product output. Because consumers apply successive increments of refined-product output to successively lower priorities of usage and because the costs of producing products may increase with output, the value of crude oil to refiners declines as its use increases. Thus, refiners are induced to purchase more crude oil only if its price declines. If the price of crude oil is the world price, P_0, U.S. refiners will purchase Q_0. If the entitlements subsidy lowers the price perceived by refiners to P_1, Q_1 is purchased and imports increase by Q_1–Q_0.

As far as the nation's economy is concerned, efficiency in the use of crude oil requires that the price paid by the nation to acquire a barrel of crude oil not exceed the value that consumers place on the contribution of that crude oil to the refined products they desire. This condition is satisfied when Q_0 is purchased and refined by domestic refiners. Under current federal regulation, however, the entitlements subsidy induces the purchase of Q_1. This quantity has an incremental value to the economy of only P_1. To realize this value, the nation hands over P_0 (the world price) to foreign sellers of crude oil. That is, the nation gets P_1 for a price of P_0. In May 1979, for example, incremental barrels of crude oil were being acquired from foreign sources for about $18.96 ($P_0$) per barrel, but they produced added value for the nation's economy of only about $16.52 ($P_1$) per barrel (the differ-

---

[3] Data are from the U.S. Department of Energy, *Monthly Energy Review*.

FIGURE 1

The Demand-side Cost of the Entitlements Program

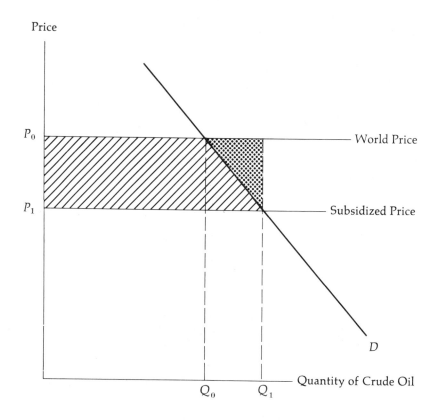

Price

P_0 — World Price

P_1 — Subsidized Price

D

Quantity of Crude Oil

Q_0 Q_1

ence being the entitlements subsidy).[4] This represents a net loss to the nation's economy. The sum of all such losses between Q_0 and Q_1 is shown by the shaded area of Figure 1.

The shaded area in Figure 1 represents the cost to the economy of the entitlements program and the demand-side gain from decontrol. It arises because refiners see the cost of crude oil to themselves as something less than the amount actually paid to foreign suppliers. Consequently, refiners use too much crude oil. Assuming that any 1 percent reduction in the price of crude oil induces refiners to increase their use of crude oil by 0.5 percent within the year of the price reduction, domestic refiners (as of May 1979) were using ap-

---

[4] U.S. Department of Energy, *Monthly Energy Review*.

proximately 375 million extra barrels of imported crude oil per year as a result of the entitlements subsidy. Of course, these extra crude-oil imports produce products of some value to the various business and individual consumers of oil. An aggregate measure of the benefit of the entitlements subsidy can be shown by the cross-hatched area in Figure 1. This area represents a surplus to the users of domestic petroleum—a surplus of the total amount users would have been willing to pay in order to have Q_1 over the amount they actually had to pay (that is, P_1 times Q_1) as a result of the entitlements subsidy. Based on May 1979 values, this surplus is worth approximately $13.2 billion annually.

Of course, the cost of Q_1 barrels of crude oil to the nation is based on the value-in-use of crude oil on world markets (P_0). Consequently, while crude-oil users perceive the total cost of Q_1 barrels of crude oil as the subsidized price, P_1 times Q_1, the nation as a whole incurs a cost of P_0 times Q_1. The difference between this cost and the cost perceived by crude-oil users is the sum of the cross-hatched and shaded areas in Figure 1 and, based on May 1979 values, totals approximately $13.7 billion annually. Thus, to produce a gain of $13.2 billion per year for the users of crude petroleum (that is, the cross-hatched area), a cost of $13.7 billion is incurred. The net loss of $500 million is the demand-side inefficiency already noted. The $3.3 billion difference between the $13.7 billion spent on the entitlements subsidy to uncontrolled oil and the total $17 billion windfall transfer available for such expenditures represents the amount spent on the special programs noted above.

This calculation of the demand-side costs of petroleum price regulation may in fact be an underestimate if there are costs of overdependence on imported oil, which the users of crude petroleum do not perceive when buying crude oil on world markets. These costs might be due, for example, to problems of national security associated with reliance on foreign supply sources or the risk of macroeconomic disequilibrium from sudden supply interruptions. If present, such costs can make the real cost of imported petroleum higher than the world price and raise our estimates of the demand-side waste induced by petroleum price regulation. If there is an "overdependence" cost of $1.00 per barrel of imported oil, for example, each of the 375 million barrels of extra crude-oil imports induced by the entitlements subsidy would have another $1.00 of associated cost. The total cost to the economy of the entitlements subsidy would then be close to $900 million per year.

Decontrol of domestic petroleum prices would raise the perceived cost of crude-oil use toward the true cost. The net gains to the economy from this policy change would appear over some moderate adjustment period. Immediately upon decontrol, it might be relatively difficult for petroleum users to reduce their consumption in response to higher prices. Over time, however, the necessary adjustments would be made and the gains from efficient energy use would be realized. These adjustments would allow petroleum users to offset the impact of deregulation on the buying power of their incomes and reduce the waste of overconsumption currently being encouraged by petroleum price regulation.

The Costs of Controls: Inefficiency on the Supply Side

Federal regulation of domestic petroleum prices not only induces overconsumption of crude oil in the United States; it also causes underproduction from domestic supply sources. This underproduction results in a net cost to the economy and a reduction in the aggregate wealth of the United States. Removal of current regulations would produce net supply-side gains.

Efficiency in crude-oil production requires that, for a given level of demand, the total cost of acquiring oil from both foreign and domestic sources be as low as possible. When the alternative to domestic oil is imported oil purchased at the world price, efficient use of the nation's resources requires the production of all domestic crude oil that can be acquired for a cost that does not exceed the price of foreign oil. This means that production of crude oil from any domestic field should be carried on until the incremental cost of the last unit of output is equated to the cost of imported oil. If the incremental cost of domestic oil exceeds the price of imported oil, it obviously would be possible to save on the expenditure of national resources by reducing domestic output and replacing it with imported oil. Conversely, if the incremental cost of domestic oil is less than the cost of imported oil, national resources could be saved by reducing imports and increasing domestic production. The intuition behind the criteria for efficiency should be clear: it makes little sense to hand over $18–19 to foreign oil producers for a barrel of crude oil if a comparable barrel can be acquired domestically for, say, $13–14.

Significantly, the criteria for efficiency in oil production are violated by crude-oil price controls. The federal ceilings on the prices that can be paid for lower- and upper-tier crude oil discourage producers from taking full advantage of supply sources that have production costs in excess of these ceilings—despite the existence of supplies that could be had for costs that are less than the cost incurred by the nation in importing crude oil. The analysis of the supply-side effects of price controls on crude-oil production can be extremely complicated when account is taken of the impact of controls on the intertemporal, dynamic setting of production, depletion, development, and exploration decisions. The essence of these effects, however, may be brought out with a more simplified approach. Figure 2 shows the production responses of crude-oil suppliers subject to price controls. As the price received increases, producers devote more resources to producing crude oil and to expanding output. Hence, the supply of oil, S, increases as price rises. The line S shows the incremental resource cost of each output level. If the world price of crude oil is P_0, uncontrolled domestic crude-oil prices would be bid up to, but not beyond, P_0. This price would be the incremental revenue for domestic producers and, hence, they would be willing to supply Q_0 barrels of output. That is, at Q_0, incremental revenues equal incremental costs. Alternatively, if the domestic producer is subject to a price control of P_1, production would be only Q_1. For a given level of demand for crude oil by refiners, this controls-induced reduction in domestic output is filled entirely by imports. Thus, domestic petroleum price regulation increases use of imported oil in the United States.

The cost of the control policy shown in Figure 2 can be illustrated by noting that an additional barrel of domestic crude oil could be had by increasing the domestic price to the height of S at an output of $Q_1 + 1$. The extra domestic barrel would reduce imports by one barrel and stem the outflow to foreign oil producers by an amount equal to P_0, while only using up domestic resources worth P_1*. Assuming, for example, another barrel of upper-tier oil (which sold for approximately $13.00 in mid-1979) could be had by raising the upper-tier ceiling to $13.10 and imported oil could be had at a cost of $18.00, a net saving of $4.90 could be obtained by allowing the ceiling price increase. Similar reasoning applies to increases in ceiling prices all the way up to the world price. The saving of national resources from such changes is equal to the difference in the world price and S at each output increment between Q_0 and Q_1; and the total saving would be the shaded area in Figure 2. This area is the supply-side cost of crude-oil price controls. It is the amount wasted on expenditures for imported oil.

The multitier EPCA pricing scheme for domestic crude oil violates economic criteria of efficiency insofar as it prevents the incremental costs of producing fields from equating to the price of im-

17

FIGURE 2

THE SUPPLY-SIDE COST OF PETROLEUM PRICE CONTROLS

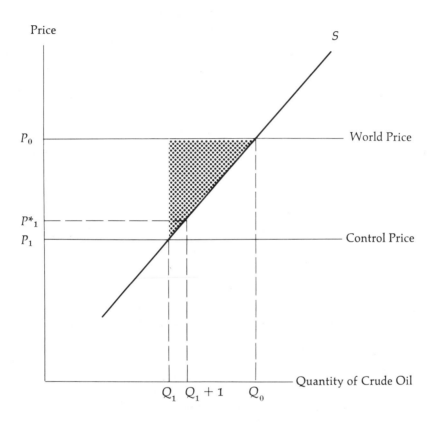

ported oil. Nevertheless, the structure of the tiered system most likely reduces the distortion relative to a system in which all domestic prices are controlled at, for example, the current domestic average. If, as seems likely, there is some range of prices over which crude oil output from newer (upper tier) fields is more responsive to price changes than output from older (lower tier) fields, the discouragement to production implied by price controls can be reduced by allowing higher prices on upper-tier oil. Moreover, the pricing provisions that allow lower-tier properties producing above base-period levels to sell incremental output at upper-tier prices provide appropriate incentives to those lower-tier fields that are fairly responsive to price increases. The stripper well provisions, on the other hand, have mixed incentives.

18

The lack of controls on stripper oil permits continued production from properties that might otherwise be shut in, but also encourages some producers perversely to *reduce* production in order to qualify for higher stripper prices. Except for this effect, the structure of the multitier controls discriminates most heavily (with lower prices) against production that responds least to such discrimination.

This observation does not imply that crude-oil price controls have no effect on domestic crude-oil output. Ceiling prices, after all, remain below market levels and any responsiveness of supply to changes in price between ceiling and world levels implies forgone domestic production. Federal petroleum price regulations discourage production of crude oil from existing domestic oil fields, as well as from fields that go unexplored or undeveloped as a result of the inability of such fields to capture a price above the upper-tier price. In the near term, both of these supply effects are potentially significant. Over the longer run, however, the discouragement of exploration and development constitutes the major source of the supply-side costs of federal crude-oil price controls, because existing fields will eventually be depleted and will cease to resemble the situation illustrated in Figure 2.

Estimates of the costs of crude-oil price controls during the period in which a supply response from existing fields is possible must account for inter-tier price differences. The supply-side costs of federal price regulation can be roughly approximated by estimating the shaded area of Figure 2 for each tier of existing production and the supply from newly developed fields. Such estimates, of course, depend on the likely responsiveness of production to decontrol. Estimates of the supply-side costs of controls are reported here under three possible assumptions concerning this responsiveness: high, medium, and low. Based on May 1979 data, the three cases are as follows:

High: Assuming existing fields show a 0.2 percent output response to every 1 percent increase in price within a year of the price increase, and new additions to producing reserves show a 0.5 percent output response within a year to every 1 percent price increase, the supply-side economic waste of crude-oil price controls amounts, on an annual basis, to approximately $2.9 billion. Controls cause the importation of roughly 830 million barrels of foreign oil per year, which would otherwise be replaced by domestic oil. These additional imports add slightly less than $16 billion to the annual bill for foreign oil.

Medium: Assuming existing fields are less responsive to price increases and show only a 0.1 percent increase in output in response to each 1 percent price increase, and new additions to producing reserves show a 0.5 percent output response within a year to every 1 percent price increase, the supply-side cost of crude-oil price controls amounts to approximately $2.0 billion per year. Additional imports of crude oil as a result of discouragement to domestic production are roughly 650 million barrels per year, causing more than a $12 billion increase in the bill for foreign oil.

Low: If oil supplies from existing fields are completely unresponsive to price increases and the only response of domestic supply to controls is in exploration and development of new fields as above, the supply-side cost of price controls is slightly over $1.1 billion per year. The encouragement to imports is roughly 500 million barrels per year, representing an addition of approximately $9 billion to the bill for imported oil.

Supply-side costs depend critically on the assumption regarding the additional supply potential in existing fields where the disparity between domestic and world price is greatest. The supply-side costs also depend on the level of the world price of oil, which influences the range over which it is efficient to produce domestically. If world oil prices continue to rise at the rate they did in the first half of 1979, the estimates reported here will understate the costs of controls. Moreover, as noted above, the multitier crude-oil price control system tends to reduce the costs of controls relative to a uniform price control system. In the medium-response case described above, for example, the supply-side cost of controls would be estimated at over $3.6 billion per year if *all* domestic crude oil were priced at the domestic average—$1.6 billion over the estimated annual costs of the actual multitier controls.

Of the possible estimates of the supply-side costs of crude-oil price controls, which is most accurate? The answer to this question depends to some extent on the period over which costs are measured. In the nearer term, the costs depend significantly on the possible responsiveness of output from existing fields to price changes. It is unlikely that there would be no response at all to decontrol. As a conservative alternative, then, the medium case can be taken as representative of reality. In this case, on the basis of the May 1979 data, the annual cost of discouraging development of new supply sources appears to be approximately $1.2 billion. In addition, the annual cost of the discouragement of production from existing supply sources appears to be approximately $0.8 billion. This latter cost would not persist because existing wells are depleted over time and new wells are allowed upper-tier prices (which are relatively close to world levels). The former cost, however, is an ongoing result of petroleum price regulation.

The costs borne by the nation as a result of continued discouragement to exploration and development and, consequently, overreliance on foreign petroleum supplies are likely to be underestimated. Controls on crude-oil prices discourage exploration and development directly by lowering their expected returns. Such price controls, however, can have more subtle effects on exploration and development activity by increasing the uncertainty of investors as to prices likely to be received in the future. Currently, newly producing oil properties qualify for upper-tier prices. Recent history, however, suggests the instability of any regulatory regime—since 1971, crude-oil prices have been subject to no less than eight pricing schemes. If investors in the exploration and development of domestic supply sources currently view the *average* domestic price (rather than the upper-tier price) as the price at which they can expect to sell their output, the annual cost of controls in terms of unrealized new supply sources would be estimated at $3.2 billion under the assumptions of the medium-response case. This is considerably larger than the $1.2 billion figure cited above. When added to the $0.8 billion cost of forgoing supplies from existing domestic sources (as estimated in the medium case), the total supply-side cost becomes $4.0 billion.

As with the demand-side inefficiency, supply-side costs of petroleum price regulation may be underestimated if there is a cost to overdependence on imported oil which raises the true cost of foreign oil above the level of the world price. Possible sources of such a cost have been mentioned above. If it is present, the cost of forgoing a barrel of domestic oil because of price controls is the difference between (1) the sum of the world price plus an overdependence premium and (2) the incremental cost of the domestic barrel. If there are, in fact, costs of dependence on imported crude oil which are not reflected in the world price, each barrel of domestic oil that is not produced is even more costly to the nation than Figure 2 implies.

In summary, the supply-side costs of petroleum price regulation arise because these regulations discourage domestic oil production and encourage the use of greater amounts of imported crude oil. These costs are realized in the form of a wasting of the nation's wealth in the sense that price controls cause the United States to hand over more dollars to foreign oil suppliers than would be necessary to satisfy any given level of demand in an uncontrolled market. This is so because a range of output from domestic sources is foreclosed by price controls but is available at incremental costs below the incremental cost of imported oil. Straightforward estimates of the annual supply-side waste range from $1.1 billion to $2.9 billion. These estimates, however, are likely to understate the costs of controls if petroleum price regulation compounds the uncertainty inherent in exploration and development and if the cost to the nation of imported oil exceeds the world price as a result of the risks associated with dependence on foreign suppliers. The avoidance of the supply-side costs of petroleum price regulation would represent a net benefit to the economy. This net gain, moreover, is conceptually distinct from the intra-economy distributional consequences of decontrol, which are discussed below, in Chapter 4.

Other Costs of Price Regulation

The analysis so far has focused on those costs of federal petroleum price regulation that arise as direct effects of this regulation on petroleum demand and supply. Costs other than the measurable overconsumption of imported oil and the underproduction of domestic oil, however, are not insignificant. These other costs include the expense of regulatory administration, enforcement, and compliance; costs associated with the implicit regulatory support for the OPEC cartel and its pricing objectives; and impairments to the economy's ability to adjust to sharp increases in world energy prices.

Administration, Enforcement, and Compliance. Discussions of the costs and benefits of regulatory policies often overlook the costs of carrying out such policies. These costs arise because resources in both the governmental and the private sectors, which might be productively devoted to other tasks, must be applied to the problems of administering, enforcing, and complying with any regulatory program. Removal of petroleum price regulations would avoid not only current inefficiencies in the consumption and production of petroleum but also the waste of resources currently devoted to the regulatory effort. The freeing of these resources would produce a net gain for the economy— a net addition to the production of the goods and services the public desires. Unfortunately, a detailed study of the costs of carrying out the current program of petroleum price regulation is confounded by the variety of forms, sometimes unmeasurable, that these costs take.

Nevertheless, evidence on some of these costs is available and suggestive of the magnitude of the resource expenditure involved.

The administrative burden of the price regulation program falls directly on two groups: the participants in the regulated market and the taxpayer. For the regulated industry, whose regulation-related costs may ultimately be borne in greatest part by consumers of petroleum products, the burdens of regulation arise from: (1) the administrative costs of maintaining records and reporting required information; (2) the disruption of normal business practices by the mandated need for federal approval; and (3) the shifting of the arena in which competitive viability is determined from the marketplace toward the political and bureaucratic realm. Evidence on some part of the first of these costs was released by a special Presidential Task Force in 1977.[5] In fiscal year 1977, the federal compliance program imposed record-keeping and reporting requirements on more than 300,000 firms. These firms are conservatively estimated to have had to file more than a million periodic, one-time, and occasional reports. The value of the man-hours devoted to this effort is estimated to have been approximately $160 million. In addition to the actual filing of reports, administrative costs are incurred to maintain records, monitor regulatory compliance, and ensure adequate representation in the attorneys' arena of exceptions, appeals, and litigation. The Presidential Task Force estimated that the sum of these costs and direct reporting costs approached $500 million in fiscal year 1977.

The presence of regulation in petroleum markets has had widespread effects on normal business practices. In many cases, the alteration of these practices has the effect of distorting the efforts of profit-seeking firms to minimize costs. Numerous aspects of refinery operations, for example, including capacity changes, shutdown for maintenance, and sale of a refinery, require either regulatory approval or clarification of regulatory obligations, because refining operations have pricing, entitlement, and buyer–supplier obligations associated with them. Similarly, transactions involving crude-oil producers require extensive certification as to quantity of production and applicability of price ceilings; and changes in many aspects of their buyer–supplier relationships with pipelines and refiners are subject to lengthy review, exception, and appeal processes. These impediments to doing business imposed by regulation raise the costs of transactions in petroleum markets.

---

[5] Paul W. MacAvoy, ed., *Federal Energy Administration: Report of the Presidential Task Force*, American Enterprise Institute: Ford Administration Papers on Regulatory Reform (Washington, D.C.: American Enterprise Institute, 1977), preface and pp. 39-54.

Some of the costs of carrying out current petroleum price regulations arise through the effects of these regulations on the forms of productivity and rivalry conducive to firms' survival and profit opportunities. As a result of the regulatory process, the viability of a firm depends relatively more than it otherwise would on its ability to "produce" favorable regulation and rulings—as opposed to its ability to produce crude oil, refined products, or marketing services. A premium can be expected to be placed, for example, on management personnel who know relatively more about getting along with and influencing regulators than about producing products for their customers. In general, the presence of a regulatory mechanism, which has the ability to shift large amounts of wealth among competing interest groups and which is subsidized by the general taxpayer, can be expected to lead interested parties to devote more resources than they otherwise would to lobbying, campaigning, and appealing for favorable regulatory decisions. Distortions of these types from the normal behavior of market participants are undoubtedly subtle and pervasive in the current environment. They are also undoubtedly costly in terms of the resources they consume.

The administrative burden on the taxpayer is also a cost of the control program. The Department of Energy (DOE) has an estimated budget for 1979 of approximately $9.6 billion and employs over 19,000 people. Of course, not all of these resources are used in the administration of petroleum price regulations. This task is the primary function of the Economic Regulatory Administration (ERA) within DOE. The direct budget allocation of the Economic Regulatory Administration is close to $130 million for 1979. If the share of the Economic Regulatory Administration in the administrative expenses of DOE's energy information, policy, and regulation programs is equal to ERA's share in the direct expenses of these programs, the measured tax burden of the ERA would show an addition of close to $80 million in 1979. Thus, the federal tax burden of current ERA regulation is in the area of $210 million annually.[6] Although not all of this tax burden would be avoided by deregulating petroleum prices (because the ERA administers programs other than petroleum price controls), a large portion of it could be eliminated.

Regulation and Higher World Oil Prices. Another source of unmeasurable costs associated with federal regulation of petroleum prices

---

[6] U.S. Office of Management and Budget, *The Budget of the United States Government: Fiscal Year 1980* (Washington, D.C., 1979), p. 129. Fiscal-year budget authorities have been converted to calendar-year figures in the text.

arises because current policies indirectly support the OPEC cartel and its pricing policies. This cartel has exercised a large degree of monopolistic control over world oil prices in the 1970s. The results are higher prices and a transfer of wealth from energy-consuming to energy-producing nations. The publicly stated U.S. policy objective prompted by these results has been energy independence. In fact, the effects of petroleum price regulations have been exactly the opposite of the professed goal.

The preceding analysis of supply- and demand-side costs has assumed that the world price of oil is invariant with respect to any actions by the United States. In Figures 1 and 2, for example, the United States is represented as being able to buy as much crude oil as it wants at a constant world price of P_0. This assumption may not be warranted (and may lead to an underestimation of the costs of controls). The net effects of both the crude-oil entitlements program and the crude-oil price control program are to encourage the importation of foreign crude oil and to encourage higher world oil prices— albeit to an unknown degree. The reduction in domestic petroleum production in the United States, which results from price controls, yields a reduction in the U.S. contribution to world supplies and thus tends to raise uncontrolled world oil prices by reducing the competition faced by OPEC oil. This upward pressure on uncontrolled crude-oil prices is reinforced by the entitlements subsidy to the use of uncontrolled crude oil. With a subsidized demand and reduced domestic production, the United States enters the world market for crude oil with a greater demand than it would have in the absence of regulation. Foreign sellers of crude oil are the beneficiaries.

The extent of any regulation-induced increase in the price of world oil is difficult to determine—particularly because it depends upon the response of the somewhat inscrutable OPEC cartel. Yet to the extent that such increases do exist, they exacerbate the adverse effects of rising world energy prices. In terms of the analysis above, each barrel of domestic production that is forgone as a result of price controls and each barrel of imported oil that is demanded as a result of entitlements subsidies may cause incremental increases in the world price of crude oil. If so, the estimates of the domestic supply- and demand-side costs of petroleum price regulation would have to be increased. The effects on world oil prices of discarding this regulation would be a gain to the United States.

Adjusting to Price Shocks. A final source of costs to petroleum price regulation lies in the domestic economy's impaired ability under price controls to adjust efficiently and rapidly to sudden changes in world energy markets. Changes in prices and profits in unregulated markets serve as the necessary informational signals and inducements that allow producers and consumers to adjust their behavior rationally when shocks to their environment occur. The efficient, resource-saving domestic response to a sudden dramatic increase in world oil prices, for example, is to increase domestic production, reduce imports, and reduce consumption. So long as the incremental cost of domestic output is below the world price, allowing domestic production to push out imports results in a net savings for the domestic economy. Similarly, allowing rising prices to reduce consumption avoids the costs associated with having petroleum put to uses that are less valuable than the incremental cost on the world market. Current federal regulatory policies inhibit the efficacy of adjustment to shocks and increase the likelihood of undesired economic disequilibria.

Controls on petroleum prices also magnify the supply-side problems of adjusting to sudden world price increases by reducing private incentives to stockpile as insurance against such increases. In an unregulated market, the prospect of an increase in world oil prices or a cutback in supply induces stockpiling behavior because such shocks imply that stockpiles of petroleum will fetch high prices during the foreign supply reduction. At least in the case of short-term supply reductions, such behavior has the beneficial effects of increasing supplies and moderating price increases over the adjustment period. Domestic price controls, of course, prevent stockpiles from fetching higher prices and, hence, discourage stockpiling. The result is a further exacerbation of the economy's adjustment problems.

Summary: Efficiency Effects of Oil Price Controls

Proposals for the deregulation of petroleum prices are often met with claims that decontrol will cost billions of dollars. Insofar as such claims are meant to refer to the distributional consequences of decontrol for some domestic interest group, they may be valid. Insofar as such claims are meant to refer to the aggregate U.S. economy, however, they are incorrect. Federal petroleum price regulations impose a net loss on the U.S. economy. The total value of goods and services available to the U.S. public is reduced by these regulations.

The net economic costs of petroleum price regulations arise from several sources. On the demand side, every barrel of crude oil now imported produces goods and services that are worth less to the American public than the cost of acquiring the oil from foreign sellers.

26

This perverse behavior is the consequence of the continuing subsidization of imported crude oil. The annual waste that results is estimated (on the basis of May 1979 data) to be approximately $500 million.

On the supply side, petroleum price regulations discourage domestic production and encourage the importation of foreign oil. Every extra barrel of oil that is imported could be replaced by output that uses national resources worth less than the payment made to the sellers of foreign oil. Failure to do this imposes a loss on the economy. This loss is conservatively estimated to be $2.0 billion annually. Over the longer run, increasing the uncertainty of investors may impose even larger costs by discouraging substantial exploration and development. Taking account of this effect, the supply-side costs of current policies could be amounting to as much as $4.0 billion annually.

Other significant costs also accompany petroleum price regulation. Both the supply- and demand-side costs, for example, are increased to the extent there are costs arising from dependence on foreign suppliers of crude petroleum. Moreover, private-sector costs of carrying out the administrative obligations created by current regulations may be as much as $500 million annually—and this estimate overlooks the costs created by distortions in business transactions and competitive behavior. The federal administrative burden of regulation on taxpayers may be over $200 million annually. More subtle costs of petroleum price regulation arise from the unambiguous support the program provides, by discouraging domestic production and subsidizing imports, for OPEC and its high world oil prices. Finally, the inflexibility and inefficiency of current policies magnify the problems the economy faces in adjusting to sudden shocks to world energy prices and supplies.

The total cost from all of these sources is uncertain; the measurable costs alone are at least in the range of $3 billion per year. These are real *net* costs incurred by our economy. Failure to take note of these costs will not improve U.S. energy policy. Nevertheless, the mere recognition of these costs is unlikely to be a sufficient base for major policy change. While removal of petroleum price controls would avoid current inefficiencies, it would have unavoidable distributional consequences. Assessment of such consequences introduces equity considerations. We now turn to an examination of this aspect of energy policy.

4
Regulation and Equity

Distributional Effects of Price Controls

A central concern of many of the policy makers who are charged with shaping U.S. energy price regulations is undoubtedly the fairness of the redistributions of income likely to accompany alternative approaches. In particular, current policy debates force a comparison of income distributions under present regulations with the prospective income distributions that would result from raising the domestic prices of oil for producers and consumers to world levels. In broad terms, three groups have a distributional stake in the outcome of impending oil pricing decisions: crude-oil producers, intermediate users of crude oil (notably refiners), and final consumers of crude oil. For the most part, the distributional interests of these groups are in conflict. In fact, even within groups, distributional interests are not identical.

As noted, rising world oil prices in the 1970s augur an increase in the wealth of domestic producers of crude oil. In the absence of the restraining effect of price controls, rising world oil prices would induce domestic producers to expand their production until their incremental costs were equated to the higher world prices—in accord with the criteria of efficiency discussed in Chapter 3. Even output from oil wells that were producing prior to the recent price increases (output that was available at previously lower incremental costs) would have its price bid up to world levels. The increased value of this output is not due to the expense of its production, but rather is the result of a windfall price increase arising from the unanticipated actions of OPEC. The result is the creation of windfall gains, or "rents," for crude-oil producers who own inframarginal supply sources. As these supply sources are exhausted, however, the windfalls evaporate.

The windfall gains that accrue to crude-oil producers as a result of rising world oil prices are a windfall loss to the consumers of crude oil. Of course, petroleum may be consumed directly or indirectly. While automobile drivers and homeowners, for example, are direct consumers of gasoline and heating oil, they are by no means the only consumers adversely affected by higher oil prices. Purchasers of energy in the industrial, commercial, and transportation sectors also face higher oil prices, and these prices raise production costs. The effects are felt as declines in the wealth of stockholders in these sectors to the extent market pressures prevent increased production costs from being passed along in the prices of final goods and services; the effects are felt as burdens by final consumers to the extent energy cost increases are reflected in the prices they ultimately pay for industrial, commercial, and transportation goods and services.

The incidence of oil or other energy price increases in thus much wider than might be inferred from simply examining direct energy consumption. In general, the effect of this observation is to make the distribution of the burden of higher prices more nearly equal across income classes than might be thought by looking at direct expenditures alone. Available evidence on the direct and indirect consumption of energy indicates that total expenditures on energy make up a slowly decreasing proportion of income as income increases, while direct expenditures are a rapidly decreasing proportion of income as income rises. Hence, the burden of energy price increases falls somewhat, but not a great deal, more heavily on poor consumers than on rich consumers.[1]

While there is some slight variation in the burden of energy price increases across income classes, there is considerable variation within income classes. Those who live in cold climates or in nonurban areas, for example, tend to spend more than others for heating residences and driving automobiles. These direct expenditures are offset to some extent because, within an income class, such consumers necessarily spend less on other goods, which have prices reflecting indirect energy content. Similarly, urban dwellers may tend to spend less on direct energy use, but consume products, such as public transportation, that have large indirect energy components. On balance, the burden of rising energy prices can be expected to be more severe for consumers

---

[1] R. Herendeen and J. Tanaka, "Energy Cost of Living," *Energy*, vol. 1, no. 2, (June 1976).

who spend more on direct energy use—regardless of their particular income levels.

This last conclusion carries important implications for the formation of energy policy. The direct use of energy, particularly for heating and industrial purposes, tends to be concentrated regionally—imparting a regional pattern to the distributional effects of rising energy prices. The geographic pattern of representation in Congress gives these effects considerable political expression. Thus, interregional differences in the distribution of burdens may influence the direction of policy even more than do the differences that exist between income classes.

The burden of rising energy prices on the users of energy induces compensating adjustment in consumption behavior. As seen above, efficiency in such adjustments requires reductions in energy use, and, in particular, the exclusion of those uses that have incremental values lower than the cost the nation incurs in acquiring energy on world markets. These adjustments take the form of reductions in the energy intensiveness of production processes and consumption patterns. Firms, industries, and sectors of the economy most able to make such adjustments over time will find themselves with relative competitive advantages. Final consumers most able to make such adjustments over time will find their real incomes less vulnerable to erosion. Over the long run, the burden of rising energy prices is most severe for users whose behavior is least responsive to price changes.

The burden of rising oil prices is particularly severe for one industry—crude-oil refining. The depressing effects of rising prices on the demand for petroleum products tend to leave current refining capacity underutilized and to discourage industry expansion. Moreover, the depressing effects of rising prices on demand tend to prevent the industry from passing on the full amount of any crude-oil price increases. The result is a decline in the value of assets in the refining sector. Over time, the exhaustion and exit of capacity and the writing down of asset values in the industry could be expected to restore rates of return. Nevertheless, some of the burden of crude-oil price increases, most likely a significant part, rests on the owners (stockholders) of oil refineries rather than on the final consumers of gasoline, heating oil, industrial fuel, and the many other refined-petroleum products.

Needless to say, the users of crude oil, both consumers and refiners, do not welcome increases in world oil prices. It is to be expected that these users of crude oil will attempt to exercise their political influence to prevent, forestall, or otherwise avoid the distributional effects of such increases. But the foregoing discussion makes it clear that the political struggle over the distributional effects of rising oil prices cannot be naively represented as a struggle between "consumers" and "the oil companies." Such a representation overlooks the fundamental divergence of interests between the oil companies that are primarily refiners and the oil companies that are primarily crude-oil producers. While such a representation undoubtedly has value as a tactic of political debate, it obscures a more subtle reality.

As we have seen, federal energy policy in the 1970s has prevented domestic crude-oil producers from capturing a large portion of the prospective windfall from OPEC's pricing actions in world markets. The beneficiaries of this policy have been the users of crude oil. Table 3 summarizes the distributional effects of federal petroleum price regulations. These estimates, which are annual values based on May 1979 data, reflect the impact of EPCA regulation in the absence of any moves toward gradual decontrol (that is, Table 3 assumes that decontrol is blocked by Congress). Moreover, Table 3 excludes the effects of the "other costs" of administration, enforcement, overdependence on imports, and so forth, which were discussed above. Inclusion of these other costs, were they all measurable, would reduce the apparent gains of consumers and refiners shown in Table 3.

The removal of crude-oil price controls would allow crude-oil producers to sell their current output at world prices. As shown in the table, the annual cost to crude-oil producers of constraints on their prices is approximately $19 billion. Without having to increase their output, crude-oil producers would capture $17 billion as a windfall from OPEC's actions were it not for controls. Moreover, by increasing their output (under the medium response case described in Chapter 3) crude-oil producers could realize another gain of $2.0 billion (the shaded area of Figure 2). This gain would not require a transfer from consumers or refiners, but would arise solely from elimination of the supply-side waste of controls. As described above, the $17 billion windfall withheld from crude-oil producers is used to finance the entitlements program. Approximately $3.3 billion of the available $17 billion is used to fund the special programs noted in Table 3. Another $13.2 billion is transferred to crude-oil users, and the remaining $0.5 billion is wasted through the demand-side inefficiency of the entitlements subsidy.

Of the $3.3 billion being spent on special programs, approximately $1.2 billion is granted as a special subsidy to small refiners,

TABLE 3

ESTIMATED DISTRIBUTIONAL EFFECTS OF CRUDE-OIL PRICE REGULATION
COMPARED WITH THE ABSENCE OF REGULATION
(billions of dollars annually as of May 1979)

Aspects of Regulation Policy	Petroleum Consumers	Petroleum Refiners	Crude-Oil Producers
Crude Oil Subsidy	+$7.3	+$5.9	−$13.2
Small Refiner Bias*	0	+ 1.2	− 1.2
Exceptions and Appeals*[a]	0	+ 0.9	− 0.9
Industrial Fuel Import Subsidy*	+ 0.6	− 0.1	− 0.5
Strategic Petroleum Reserve Subsidy*[b]	+ 0.1	0	− 0.1
21¢ Allowance to Refiners	0	+ 0.6	− 0.6
Demand-Side Inefficiency	0	0	− 0.5
Supply-Side Inefficiency (medium case)[c]	0	0	− 2.0
Total	+$8.0	+$8.5	−$19.0

* Indicates estimate based on preliminary data.

[a] Includes estimates of miscellaneous special allocations of entitlements, such as those made to imports of certain refined products and the use of California crude oil.

[b] It is assumed here that in the absence of the Strategic Petroleum Reserve subsidy, equivalent revenues would be raised through taxes on the general public. Consumers of petroleum products come closest to representing the general public. See text for further discussion.

[c] See Chapter 3 for a description of the medium-supply response case.

$0.9 billion is distributed to refiners through exceptions and appeals, $0.5 billion is spent to subsidize imports of industrial fuel, $0.1 billion goes to the Strategic Petroleum Reserve, and $0.6 billion accrues to refiners from the 21-cents-per-barrel allowance granted to them in selling entitlements. Most of the benefits of these special programs are pure transfers to the refining industry. The industrial fuel import subsidy, however, directly reduces the incremental cost of imported fuel and can be expected to be reflected in lower prices for industrial consumers. This reduction is equivalent to an annual transfer of roughly $0.6 billion to users of industrial fuel. Of this $0.6 billion, $0.5 billion is being directly financed by the entitlements program and the remainder is transferred by reducing domestic prices, to the detriment of domestic refiners. This effect costs the domestic refining sector approximately $0.1 billion. Finally, determination of the incidence of the $0.1 billion subsidy to the Strategic Petroleum Reserve is particularly problematic. Were it not financed out of the windfall rents associated with crude oil, this subsidy might be financed through taxes on the general public, oil consumers, refiners, or crude-oil producers. As a likely case, Table 3 assumes the subsidy would be raised from the general public. If requisite taxes were roughly proportional to income, and energy consumption is roughly proportional to income, the incidence of the subsidy can be approximately assigned to consumers.

The entitlements crude-oil subsidy is financed by the $13.7 billion difference between the $17 billion spent on all components of the entitlements program and the amount spent on the special programs component. As noted, the demand-side inefficiency associated with this subsidy is estimated to be worth $0.5 billion. The remaining $13.2 billion is the value of the subsidy to the users of crude oil. The users of crude oil, however, include both refiners and consumers; and their division of the $13.2 billion transfer is not self-evident. As already noted, the entitlements subsidy lowers incremental refining costs and encourages an expansion of the domestic refining industry. This cost reduction and expansion places downward pressure on the prices the various consumers pay for refined petroleum products. The result is a pass-through of some portion of the entitlements subsidy.

Estimation of the magnitude of the entitlements subsidy pass-through plays a crucial role in the analysis of the distributional effects of federal petroleum price regulation and the propriety of any change in this regulation. For example, in the limiting case of a full pass-through of the entitlements subsidy, refined petroleum product prices would be held down by approximately 5.8 cents per gallon relative to the uncontrolled market; and consumers would receive the entire $13.2 billion entitlements transfer. However, a complete pass-through to consumers is unlikely because of both the upward pressure on refining costs of expansion within the refining industry (induced by the entitlements subsidy) and the negative relationship between the demands for petroleum products and their prices. At the other extreme (as some analysts have argued), virtually none of the entitlements subsidy may be passed on in the form of lower refined-product prices. This could arise, for example, if domestic refiners face direct competition from imported refined products and the subsidy-induced domestic expansion is insufficient to cause a decline in world refined-product prices.[2] If the entitlements subsidy fails to reduce product

---

[2] See, for example, Charles E. Phelps and Rodney T. Smith, *Petroleum Regulation: The False Dilemma of Decontrol* (Santa Monica, Calif.: Rand Corporation, January 1977).

Shambaugh Library

prices, consumers are not benefiting from the system of petroleum price controls, and decontrol would therefore have no impact on them. This limiting case, however, like the case of complete pass-through, does not appear to be consistent with available evidence.

Most evidence (including the degree to which the United States is insulated from world refined-product markets and the ability of U.S. production to affect world product prices) indicates that a considerable portion of the entitlements subsidy is channeled to petroleum-product consumers. An average pass-through of around 40 percent across all products appears most likely. Nevertheless, because much of the debate concerning the retention or removal of crude-oil price controls centers on the effects of these policy options on consumers, it would be inappropriate in the present analysis to make assumptions that falsely minimize the size of such effects. Accordingly, in order to err, if we must, in a direction that makes decontrol appear less palatable, Table 3 assumes a 55 percent pass-through of the entitlements subsidy. This figure is a high estimate, but it is not absolutely inconsistent with available evidence.[3] With a 55 percent pass-through, roughly $7.3 billion (3 cents per gallon) of the crude-oil subsidy is passed on to petroleum-product users. Approximately $5.9 billion is retained by refiners. With a 40 percent pass-through, the gains of consumers and refiners from the entitlements subsidy would be $5.3 billion and $7.9 billion, respectively.

When the distributional effects of the special programs are added to those of the crude-oil subsidy in Table 3, the total transfers to consumers and refiners amount to $8.0 billion and $8.5 billion per year, respectively. The combined $16.5 billion annual gain of these interest groups, however, is less than the cost of current policy for crude-oil producers. This observation is, in fact, a restatement of the conclusion that current policies are inefficient and produce net economic waste. If oil prices are allowed to rise to world levels, the size of the nation's economic "pie" will increase by $2.5 billion—the difference between the gain to crude-oil producers and the loss to crude-oil users. Moreover, the gainers could hypothetically compensate the losers from decontrol by paying the losers their losses while still leaving themselves better off. In fact, it is possible to make everyone better off by decontrolling oil prices and paying sufficient compensation to those who would face higher prices.

---

[3] Joseph P. Kalt, "Federal Regulation of Petroleum Prices: A Case Study in the Theory of Regulation," doctoral dissertation, University of California at Los Angeles, forthcoming 1979.

Faced with a choice between continued price controls and decontrol coupled with an appropriate compensation scheme, there appear to be no clear grounds in terms of efficiency or equity for preferring the former alternative. For example, a perfectly designed windfall-profits tax and redistribution scheme, which leaves the incremental production and consumption incentives of the unregulated market unaffected, could accompany decontrol and satisfy the compensation objective. Such a scheme, however, is a practical impossibility because of such problems as distinguishing between truly *windfall* profits on inframarginal output and profits that arise from optimal adaptation to a changing world energy market.

In the absence of compensation of the losers by the gainers from a given regulatory change designed to improve efficiency, policy makers typically face a trade-off between the anticipated efficiency gains and the equity implications of improving the well-being of one group at the expense of another. Indeed, if compensation does not occur, improvements in economic efficiency constitute sufficient justification for policy action only for the rare policy maker who finds all improvements in society-wide efficiency to be equitable regardless of their effects on the many individual members of society. For most policy makers, perceptions of injustice are likely to temper their willingness to support such policy changes. It is consequently appropriate to examine the implications of alternative standards of equity—particularly because forthcoming oil pricing proposals are unlikely to be tied to compensation schemes. It is most relevant here to consider the equity implications of decontrolling oil prices. The major distributional effects of such a move, of course, are indicated by reversing "minus" and "plus" signs in Table 3.

Equity and Decontrol

While economists are fairly successful at defining criteria of efficiency, they have no special skill in defining criteria of justice. The latter task is the realm of the philosopher and moral theorist. Even among such theorists, however, general agreement is scarce. Consequently, the equity implications of decontrol are considered here from the point of view of several alternative and fairly widely held conceptions of distributional propriety. We consider, in order, standards of efficiency-based equity, voluntarism in the exchange of property, horizontal equity, regional equity, and vertical equity.

Efficiency-based Equity Standards. We have already touched on this approach to problems of fairness in policy making. This hard-boiled approach recommends that only the effect on economic efficiency be considered in evaluating any particular policy and that the distributional effects of the policy be excluded from policy decisions. If the income distribution in society must be a subject of public policy, remedial redistributions should, at best, be accomplished through nondistortive head taxes or, at worst, through the general income tax and welfare systems. In this view, it is improper to attempt to carry out redistributional goals under the cover of energy policy—particularly when the repercussions of distortions in markets as important as the energy markets are likely to have extremely undesirable effects on the efficiency of the economy. The holders of this point of view should unambiguously support decontrol of oil prices.

Voluntarism in Exchange. This view takes the freedom of the individual as its basic standard of equity in judging the propriety of any policy move. In particular, it regards the rights of individuals to voluntarily engage in exchange as inviolate and, thus, would regard as unjust coercion current prohibitions on the ability of crude-oil producers to take their oil to the marketplace and exchange it with the highest willing bidders.

The voluntarist's general approach to what is proper in the realm of governmental policy is, of course, embodied in many of the protections to individual freedom contained in our civil, criminal, and contract law; and the objections most commonly made in response to this approach arise from concerns over its possible effects on income distribution—the equity bases for which are discussed below. Notwithstanding such objections, any holder of the voluntarist-based standards of equity described here should unambiguously support the decontrol of oil prices.

Horizontal Equity. This view holds that those who were alike before a change should be alike after a change. Thus, for example, this view would argue that because a rise in gasoline prices has a more adverse impact on commuters and rural residents, who use their cars more extensively than city-dwellers, commuters and rural residents should, after a gasoline price change, receive compensation sufficient to restore their positions relative to city-dwellers. Such compensation, however, is extremely difficult to carry out. Requisite measurements made before a price change are rarely available, and measurements made after a change are negated by the prospect of compensation itself (which induces behavior designed to qualify for greater compensation). Moreover, horizontal equity based upon a given historical context is likely to discriminate heavily in favor of present and against future conditions. Specifically, if existing consumers are granted exclusive rights to a continued supply of oil from low-cost sources, new consumers entering the market will be confined to high-cost alternatives. In such a case, horizontal equity is not preserved between actual and potential market participants.

Notwithstanding these problems with the concept of horizontal equity, the proponent of such a guide to policy formation would most probably favor the regulation of petroleum prices on grounds of fairness, but would face a difficult trade-off between this equity judgment and the continuation of the inefficiencies created by oil price controls. Removal of these inefficiencies would raise the possibility of increasing everyone's well-being, yet the inefficiencies may be considered tolerable because controls tend to keep prices closer to the levels that existed prior to the quadrupling of world oil prices. Thus controls tend to maintain horizontal equity among users according to the intensiveness of their energy use. Decontrol might have minor effects on the structure of relative prices, but its effect on the level of prices would upset horizontal equity between those who use greater amounts of energy or who are less responsive to price changes and those who consume less energy or who are more responsive to price changes. Decontrol coupled with a compensation scheme designed to maintain horizontal equity would be hopelessly complex —the expense of administration would undoubtedly be tremendous.

Regional Equity. This view holds, in effect, that certain individuals are more deserving of income than other individuals on the basis of their geographic location. Holding other things (such as income levels and living conditions) equal, this view might still express a preference, for example, for redistributions from the South to the North on equity grounds. In the case of oil price regulation, a proponent of regional equity with a bias for "Northeastness" would most likely oppose decontrol because energy use (particularly of industrial fuel) is higher in that region than elsewhere and its energy users would bear a larger portion of the consumer burden from decontrol. Conversely, a preference for "Southwestness" would most likely lead a policy maker to favor decontrol in view of the geographical concentration of crude-oil deposits. Discrimination on the basis of regional origin or location, however, is analytically the same as discrimination on the basis of race, age, hair color, or other similar characteristics.

To be sure, the regional pattern of the distributional effects of decontrol would be somewhat uneven. This uneven pattern might exacerbate problems of poverty in a given region and serve as justification for offsetting policy measures. The regional bias of such measures, however, would be based on criteria of equity in the distribution of income, rather than a standard of regional equity. The former criteria may be more easily defended.

Vertical Equity. Perhaps the most commonly invoked notion of equity in policy deliberations is that of vertical equity. In this view, the crucial issue of concern in discussions of fairness is the distribution of income among individuals. The individual is the unit of analysis, and considerations such as region of residence are irrelevant. All individuals are equal in the sense that a transfer between individual A and individual B that moves A to B's income and *vice versa* would be judged distributionally neutral, that is, neither approved nor condemned by the standard of vertical equity.

The attribute of the distribution of income that is typically cited as the proper standard by which to judge the justness of any change is equality: the more nearly equal the distribution of income, the more just it is. This egalitarianism may be derived in a utilitarian context from the assumption that the contributions to any individual's well-being of incremental additions to income diminish as total income increases. It may also be derived from an implicit consensus of rational individuals supporting relief for those who are worse off. The measure of individual welfare, however, is absolute income rather than relative income—judgments of equity are not based on envy. Thus, a change that improves the income of an already wealthy individual would be, in itself, equitable; but such a change would raise the issue of possible redistribution of the change in income to a poor individual, which would be even more equitable.

From this viewpoint, the equalization of incomes through redistribution is limited only by the disincentives to production that are likely to arise. Inequality of abundance is preferred to equality of misery. Because available instruments for redistribution, such as taxes and transfer payments, tend to reduce the gains from risk-taking and intensive forms of labor service, there is ultimately a trade-off between equality and abundance.

A fairly straightforward statement can be made of the utilitarian criterion of vertical equity, which embodies recognition of the trade-off between equality and efficiency: a dollar of income received by a rich person is not without value in equity assessments, but it is not as valuable as a dollar received by a poor person. If a policy measure can redirect income downward in the income scale with no adverse effects on production incentives, it is approved by the utilitarian criterion. A policy measure that redistributes income downward but reduces total output in the economy (so that the amount taken away from the rich is greater than the amount delivered to the poor) is justified if and only if the value assigned by the utilitarian criterion to the dollars transferred to the poor is not less than the value assigned by the utilitarian criterion to the dollars lost by the rich.

Under this formulation of a standard of fairness, it is possible to make an explicit comparison of the efficiency and equity effects of decontrolling oil prices. To do so, several assumptions are necessary. Most important, it is assumed that the incremental contribution of a dollar of income to a utilitarian measure of equity is inversely proportional to the present income of the recipient. Thus, for example, it is half as valuable to give a dollar to an individual with an income of $20,000 as it is to give a dollar to an individual with an income of $10,000. It is also assumed that the consumption of energy is proportional to income. Moreover, dollar transfers from or to industries are taken here as being transfers from or to the stockholders of those industries. The only redistributions assumed to be relevant to equity considerations are those occurring between consumers and crude-oil producers; redistributions among different industries, such as between refiners and crude-oil producers, are treated as distributionally neutral because the stockholders of different industries tend to have the same incomes.

The key empirical fact in the analysis of the equity consequences of decontrol is that the distribution of stockholdings is very different from the distribution of income. Data on stockholdings in crude-oil producing and refining companies are scarce, but it is not likely to be a significant error to assume that the distribution of such stockholdings across income classes is much the same as the distribution of stockholding in general. As Table 4 indicates, general stockholding is done disproportionately by the rich.

Clearly, any policy change that takes from the general public in proportion to income and redistributes to general stockholders will cause a loss of value as measured by the utilitarian standard of vertical equity. Such a redistribution would take dollars from those who are weighted relatively heavily by this standard and transfer dollars to those who are weighted relatively lightly. For the policy maker adhering to the utilitarian standard, the resulting loss of value is a measure of inequity.

With the figures in Table 4 and the assumption that the equity value of a dollar is inversely proportional to the income of the gainer

TABLE 4

Distribution of Stockholdings by Income Class, 1971

Income Class (annual income)	Percentage of Families	Percentage of Market Value of Stock Held
Under $5,000	22.0	2.4
$5,000–9,999	31.4	7.0
$10,000–14,999	23.5	8.9
$15,000–24,999	17.3	12.8
$25,000–49,999	4.8	17.8
$50,000–99,999	0.8	20.9
$100,000 and up	0.2	30.2

Source: M. H. Blume, J. Crockett, and I. Friend, "Stockownership in the U.S.: Characteristics and Trends," *Survey of Current Business*, vol. 54, no. 11 (November 1974), table 3, p. 26.

or loser, it turns out that any redistribution from the general public to stockholders has an equity cost of approximately one-half the size of the transfer.[4] Thus, for example, if the decontrol of oil prices transfers 1 percent of consumers' income to crude-oil producers, the

---

[4] By the assumptions of the text, a dollar received by an individual with an income of x dollars has an equity value of $1/x$. Now we wish to compare equity values under two methods of allocating a dollar of income across income groups. The two cases are: (1) allocating an additional dollar in proportion to income (as with the transfer to consumers under continued controls), and (2) allocating an additional dollar in proportion to stockholding (as under decontrol).

In the first case, if individuals in the lowest income group receive x_1 dollars of income per person and if the fraction of the total population with an income in the lowest income group is p_1, the lowest income group will receive a fraction of a dollar allocated in proportion to income which is equal to $p_1x_1/(p_1x_1+p_2x_2+p_3x_3\ldots)$, where "2" and "3" refer to higher income groups. This fraction, however, is just $p_1x_1/\bar{x}$, where $\bar{x}$ is the average income across individuals. With the lowest income group receiving this fraction of the allocated dollar, the equity value of this group's gain would be $(p_1x_1/\bar{x})/x_1=p_1/\bar{x}$. Similarly, the transfer to the next-to-the-lowest income group would have an equity value of p_2/x, and so on for higher income groups. The total equity value of a dollar allocated in proportion to income is the sum of the equity values associated with each group: $p_1/\bar{x}+p_2/\bar{x}+p_3/\bar{x}\ldots=\$1/\bar{x}$.

In the second case, a dollar is allocated in proportion to stockholding. The equity value of a dollar so allocated depends on the fraction of stock held by each income group. Call this fraction q, so that the fraction of stock held by the lowest income group is q_1, q_2 is the fraction held by the next highest group, and so on. The lowest income group receives q_1 of a dollar allocated in proportion to stockholding, at an equity value of q_1/x_1. The total equity value of this allocation scheme is thus $q_1/x_1+q_2/x_2+q_3/x_3\ldots$. Therefore, the ratio of the equity values of a dollar allocated in proportion to income and a dollar allocated in proportion to stockholding is $(\$1/x)/(q_1/x_1+q_2/x_2+q_3/x_3\ldots)$, which is approximately 2 with the data of Table 4.

equity loss is the same as if ½ percent of everyone's income were destroyed.

Table 3 indicates that decontrol of crude-oil prices would result in a transfer of approximately $8.0 billion from the users of petroleum products to the stockholders of crude-oil producing companies. This is the transfer that concerns the utilitarian policy maker, as the transfer from refiners to crude-oil producers would be distributionally neutral.

A portion of the $8.0 billion transfer from consumers to crude-oil producers, however, would also amount to an intra-corporate-sector transfer. Only about 20 percent of domestically consumed petroleum is consumed directly by residential and commercial (small business) users, while 80 percent is consumed by the industrial, transportation, and utility sectors. Assuming nine-tenths of any change in petroleum product prices is passed on to ultimate consumers of the goods and services sold by these sectors, the transfer from decontrol that should concern the utilitarian policy maker amounts to slightly less than $7.4 billion. Of this gross total that would be transferred to crude-oil producers, federal corporate income taxes, state income taxes, and severance taxes would together capture approximately 48 percent.[5] Under the plausible assumption that resulting tax revenues would produce benefits or offset other tax collections roughly in proportion to income, a net redistribution of roughly $3.8 billion would remain. By the analysis of the weighting of equity values, this redistribution would have an equity cost of one-half of the aggregate redistribution, or $1.9 billion.

There are several factors that suggest that this is a high estimate of the equity loss of decontrol computed under the utilitarian criteria. Royalty payments to landowners by crude-oil producers, for example, are typically equivalent to a tax of approximately one-sixth of the producers' revenues. When the lands are public, royalty payments go to governmental units and may carry no equity loss. Other royalty recipients are most likely classed somewhere between stockholders and consumers in the income distribution. Thus, to the extent decontrol would cause a transfer from consumers to landowners, rather than to crude-oil producers, estimates of equity losses would have to be reduced. In addition, the assumption of distributional neutrality in redistribution from refiners to crude-oil producers may be some-

---

[5] The effective tax rate is based on Emil M. Sunley, deputy assistant secretary of the Treasury, "Statement Before the Subcommittee on Energy and Foundations of the Senate Finance Committee," *Department of the Treasury News*, May 7, 1979, table XIII.

what inaccurate. In particular, small refiners tend to be private or closely held public companies and some of their owners fall into the very highest income classes. Thus, some of the transfer from refiners to crude-oil producers would be regarded as an equity gain to be offset against the equity cost of the redistribution from consumers to crude-oil producers.

Estimates of the equity cost of decontrol based on Table 3 overlook the other costs of current policies, which are associated with private and public administrative burdens, support for OPEC pricing, impairments to the economy's ability to adjust to outside shocks, and overdependence on foreign oil. As noted above, most of these costs are difficult to measure, yet are likely to be large. Of those costs that are measurable, a significant portion undoubtedly falls on individual consumers. Assuming, for example, that three-fourths of the estimated $500 million of private administrative and compliance costs of current regulation are passed entirely on to consumers, the estimate of the equity cost of decontrol would be reduced from $1.9 billion to slightly more than $1.5 billion. Similarly, if even one-half of the Economic Regulatory Administration budget of approximately $210 million could be freed by decontrol and applied to other programs with benefits distributed roughly in proportion to income, the equity cost estimate would have to be reduced to approximately $1.4 billion. Of the costs of current policies which are not readily measurable, such as impairments to macroeconomic adjustment, alteration of normal business practices in the petroleum industry, and national security problems from increased dependence on foreign crude-oil suppliers, it is fair to conclude that many fall on the general public— and perhaps disproportionately on those with relatively low incomes. This suggests further reductions in the estimated equity cost of decontrol.

The discussion of the equity costs of decontrol makes it clear that an adherent to a utilitarian standard of vertical equity would have a difficult time measuring all of the effects of decontrol. Forced to place dollar values on these effects, estimates in the range of $1.0–1.4 billion appear to be generous, but not altogether unreasonable.[6] How does this compare with the gains from improved efficiency under decontrol? The conservative estimates of the supply- and demand-side gains in Table 3 amount to approximately $2.5 billion. Estimates based on assumptions discussed above, which make crude-

---

[6] With a 40 percent pass-through, the measurable equity cost of decontrol would only be $0.8 billion. As noted above, a 40 percent pass-through is more likely than the 55 percent pass-through assumed in Table 3.

oil supply responses to decontrol more pronounced, raise this estimate to the $4 billion range. Certainly, a $2.5–3.5 billion estimate of the supply- and demand-side gains of decontrol is not unreasonable. But within the utilitarian framework, this $2.5–3.5 billion cannot be directly compared to the $1.0–1.4 billion equity loss without specifying who would receive the gain.

The supply- and demand-side gains from decontrol would accrue to crude-oil producers, but they would *not* be received at the expense of consumers or refiners. They are *net* gains that would accrue to crude-oil producers even if compensation had to be paid to consumers and refiners. Hence, from the viewpoint of vertical equity, the efficiency gains from decontrol are not inequitable. In fact, as net gains to society, they constitute an improvement by utilitarian criteria, although (for the purposes of comparison with the equity loss resulting from the transfer of consumer wealth) the utilitarian standard would value each dollar of the efficiency gains captured by crude-oil producers at approximately one-half of a dollar. A portion of these gains, however, would be lost by crude-oil producers as a result of corporate income and severance taxes. Maintaining the same assumptions about the use of tax revenues that were made above, the $2.5–3.5 billion efficiency gain of decontrol would have a value of $1.9–2.6 billion to the utilitarian policy maker. Comparing this with the $1.0–1.4 billion equity loss, the proponent of the utilitarian standard of vertical equity should most probably support the decontrol of oil prices. Of course, from the utilitarian view, the equity gains from decontrol could be increased even further by accompanying decontrol with a windfall-profits tax that generates proceeds that offset the distributional effects of decontrol.

It is important to stress that the utilitarian policy maker's interest in coupling decontrol with a windfall-profits tax would arise from a desire to offset the regressive distributional aspects of decontrol, rather than a desire to pursue other goals such as the financing of energy research and development trust funds. Recalling that energy consumption is roughly proportional to income, the utilitarian's compensatory objectives could be accomplished by a windfall-profits tax that generates proceeds for the Treasury's general revenue fund, so long as such revenues offset other taxes or yield expenditure benefits that are approximately proportional to income. Proposals that would use windfall-profits tax revenues to subsidize energy research or similar projects are less appealing in the utilitarian context. It is unlikely, for example, that such subsidization would have a distributional pattern that comes close to offsetting the impact of decontrol on those who pay higher petroleum prices. Certainly, the direct benefits of subsidizing energy research and development would accrue to shareholders and labor in high-technology industries which produce substitutes for petroleum—and these groups have already realized substantial gains in the energy environment of this decade. Moreover, it is not true that the availability of windfall-profits tax revenues reduces the cost of undertaking the projects that would be supported by an energy trust fund. Both these revenues and the resources that would be used up by such projects have alternative valuable uses. If the benefits of trust-fund projects exceed the costs of the resources they use up and if there are no equity grounds for opposing such projects, they should be undertaken even if there were no crude-oil industry to tax as the source of funding. In short, the utilitarian's concern over the distributional consequences of decontrol are conceptually distinct from the myriad of expenditure programs that might interest policy makers. The utilitarian policy maker should most prefer decontrol with a compensatory windfall-profits tax, although decontrol by itself is still preferable to continued price regulation.

It would be inappropriate to place great confidence in the precise numerical figures by which these conclusions have been reached. The numerical estimates of losses and gains are meant to indicate the order of magnitude of the stakes in the debate over decontrol. The estimates of equity losses and gains calculated here depend on the choice of weighting schemes by which transfers to rich and poor are valued. Moreover, the estimates calculated here are dependent on our imperfect ability to measure all relevant costs and benefits. The unmeasurable other costs of current policies are given little notice in our numerical calculations. Yet, these costs are likely to be far from insignificant. If these other costs amount to only $1.4 billion per year in outlays by individual consumers, there might be no equity loss from decontrol at all. Termination of current regulations would then be even more clearly the preferred policy of utilitarian policy makers.

Summary: Equity Effects of Oil Price Decontrol

The impact of rising world energy prices is felt as a loss of income by the users of energy. Such price increases reduce the command of energy users over the real goods and services they desire. Final consumers of energy bear the distributional consequences of rising prices through their direct and indirect purchases of energy, while intermediate users of energy bear the distributional consequences of rising energy prices through increased production costs and the inability to pass through all increases in input prices. In response to the burdens of rising energy prices, of course, energy users rationally attempt to reduce their use of energy and to find alternatives to those forms of energy that have the most rapidly rising prices.

Producers of primary energy stand to gain from rising world energy prices. Producers respond rationally to these increasing prices (and capture the income they generate) by attempting to expand production. In the domestic regulatory environment of the 1970s, however, both the prospective transfers of income to crude-oil producers and the expected response in domestic energy supply have been restrained by federal price controls. Moreover, in the case of oil, the prospective transfers of income to crude-oil producers have been used to finance an elaborate program of subsidies to petroleum refiners and consumers. Consequently, much of the debate concerning the appropriate pricing of oil now centers on the equity implications of altering existing systems of controls and subsidies. In particular, the debate over continuation of federal price regulation versus decontrol forces policy makers to address the questions of fairness raised by the different distributional implications of these two alternatives.

Decontrol of oil prices would cause a redistribution of income from consumers and refiners to crude-oil producers. Whether the direction of this redistribution is considered equitable depends on the standards of social justice that the concerned policy maker brings to the analysis. Under some standards, the redistribution implied by decontrol is equitable. From these viewpoints, decontrol is unambiguously a preferred policy alternative—and this conclusion is reinforced by the magnitude of the beneficial effects of decontrol on the efficiency of the nation's economy. From many other viewpoints, however, the redistribution of income implied by decontrol is inequitable. For proponents of these views, the choice between continued regulation and decontrol is not an easy one: decontrol is considered to have unfair distributional effects, but also to produce unambiguous gains in efficiency for the economy as a whole. The attempts made here to quantify the resulting trade-off suggest how well-meaning policy makers can make a proper decision. The character of the analysis suggests that the gain from the decontrol of oil prices would outweigh the harm.

5

Conclusion

The political debate over the appropriate pricing of energy has been one of the most hotly contested of the 1970s. The prospect that the trend toward increasing scarcity and higher world prices will continue to characterize energy markets over at least the next decade suggests that this debate will not cool quickly. The political fervor that issues of energy pricing arouse should not be surprising. At stake are billions of dollars of income. These serve as the lure for political involvement and provide the incentive for interest groups to organize and exert their power. Whether the political system will produce decisions that satisfy the objectives of narrowly defined interest groups, rather than more broadly conceived standards of economic efficiency and equity, remains to be seen. Certainly, if this issue is to have a chance of being resolved in favor of the latter alternative, it is important to raise the level of analysis available to policy makers above the realm of political catch phrases.

The fundamental, but most often obscured, fact about U.S. energy policy is that many current regulations impose net costs on the nation. In the face of rising world prices, efficiency in the domestic use of energy requires two basic responses:

• Other things being equal (such as income), domestic consumers must reduce their use of energy until the lowest-valued application of energy is worth no less than the cost to the country of acquiring energy.

• Domestic producers must expand their output from domestic energy sources until the cost of domestic production is equal to the cost the country bears in acquiring foreign energy supplies.

Federal regulation of energy prices prevents the satisfaction of these conditions. In the case of oil, federal regulations keep the prices producers receive below the prices determined in world markets and subsidize the consumption of oil by presenting users with an effective domestic price below the cost of acquiring foreign oil. The results are an underproduction of domestic oil and an overconsumption of imported oil. In pursuing these policies and failing to use energy efficiently, the nation wastes billions of dollars annually.

Decontrol of oil prices would result in a net gain to the nation. This observation does not imply, however, that everyone would gain from decontrol—only that those who would benefit from decontrol would gain more than those who would be harmed by decontrol would lose. In fact, those who would gain from decontrol would gain enough to compensate fully the losers from decontrol and still be better off themselves. Of course, in the absence of compensation, this conclusion is small consolation for those who would lose from decontrol.

The users of crude oil would be the losers from decontrol. Specifically, crude-oil refiners and the intermediate and final consumers of products made from crude oil would transfer income to crude-oil producers upon removal of current regulations. This prospective redistribution of income must force the thoughtful policy maker to ask whether the effects of decontrol would be equitable. For the policy maker who does not find the redistributions implied by decontrol to be unjust, decontrol (without a windfall-profits tax) must be supported on grounds of both efficiency and equity. For the policy maker who does regard these redistributions as inequitable, however, such a policy choice is more difficult—efficiency and equity effects must somehow be weighed against each other. If the removal of price controls is accompanied by a windfall-profits tax that offsets the regressiveness of decontrol without destroying the incentives which foster efficiency, decontrol should be supported—even by the policy maker who finds the distributional consequences of decontrol to be inequitable.

Our analysis indicates that, even under standards of social justice that find the prospective transfer of income from consumers to producers highly inequitable, the efficiency gains from decontrol are dominant over the distributional losses. Consequently, with full cognizance of the distributional implications, we recommend the deregulation of domestic petroleum prices. The nation is quite simply paying too great a price for maintaining income patterns that fail to reflect the world market conditions brought on by OPEC and for trying to forestall the adjustment to a present and future of rising energy prices.